INDIAN

© 1998 Rebo International b.v., The Netherlands
1998 Rebo Productions Ltd
Photographs and recipes by Rolli Books
Typeset by MATS, Southend-on-Sea, Essex
Printed in Slovenia
Designed and created by CONSORTIUM, England
Edited by Anne Sheasby
Illustrations by Camilla Sopwith
J0239
ISBN 1 84053 0782

INDIAN

RICH AND SPICY, AUTHENTIC AND REGIONAL DISHES TO CREATE

REBO
PRODUCTIONS

Contents

Introduction

Indian cuisine is famous throughout the world for its richness and variety of flavours. Each region contributes its own unique character and flavour to the tradition, drawing from an extensive range of seasonings and spices.

In fact, the secret of Indian cuisine lies in the subtle combination of these spices and flavourings. Some have an inherently 'cooling' effect while others have 'warming' properties. In addition, many are widely believed to have beneficial qualities with regard to general health and well-being.

Basic Indian Recipes

Many of the following are used as components in recipes throughout the book.

Paneer

In a saucepan, bring 3 litres (5¼ pints) of milk to the boil. Just before the milk boils, add 90 ml (6 tbsp) of lemon juice or vinegar to curdle the milk. Strain the curdled milk through a piece of muslin to allow all the whey and moisture to drain away. Still wrapped in the muslin, place the paneer under a weight and refrigerate for 2-3 hours to allow it to set into a block. The paneer can then be cut or grated from the block.

Garlic paste and ginger paste

Soak 300 g (10½ oz) of fresh ginger or garlic cloves overnight to soften the skins. Peel and chop roughly. Process in a food processor, or pound with a pestle and mortar, until pulped. The pulp can be stored in an airtight container and refrigerated for 4-6 weeks.

Almond or cashew nut paste

Process 300 g (10½ oz) of blanched almonds or raw cashew nuts in a food processor, or pound with a pestle and mortar, with enough groundnut or vegetable oil to form a thick paste. Process or pound until fairly smooth. Refrigerate in an airtight container.

Green chilli or red chilli paste

Roughly chop the required amount of green or red chillies, and process in a food processor, or pound with a pestle and mortar, until pulped.

Raw papaya paste

Roughly chop the required amount of peeled raw papaya, and process in a food processor until smooth.

Fresh mint paste

Wash and dry the required quantity of fresh mint leaves and process in a food processor, or pound with a pestle and mortar, until a paste forms.

Mint chutney

Chop the following ingredients and process in a food processor, or pound with a pestle and mortar, until a paste forms: 60 g (2¼ oz) fresh mint leaves, 125 g (4½ oz) fresh coriander leaves, 5 ml (1 tsp) cumin seeds, 2 garlic cloves, 1 green chilli, 25 g (1 oz) mango flesh, 50 g (1¾ oz) peeled tomatoes and salt to taste. Refrigerate in an airtight container.

Garam masala

Garam masala is widely available as a ready-prepared spice mix, but it is easy to make your own and is likely to be more aromatic than the shop-bought variety.

Finely grind together the following ingredients: 90 g (3¼ oz) cumin seeds, 70 g (2½ oz) black peppercorns, 75 g (2¾ oz) black cardamom seeds, 25 g (1 oz) fennel seeds, 40 g (1½ oz) green cardamoms, 35 g (1¼ oz) coriander seeds, 20 g (¾ oz) cloves, 20 cinnamon sticks, 2.5 cm (1 in) in length, 20 g (¾ oz) ground mace, 20 g (¾ oz) black cumin seeds, 15 g (½ oz) dried rose petals, 15 g (½ oz) dried bay leaves, 15 g (½ oz) ground ginger. Store in an airtight container.

Chaat masala

Take 70 g (2½ oz) cumin seeds, 60 g (2¼ oz) black peppercorns, 25 g (1 oz) dried mint leaves, 15 ml (1 tsp) carom seeds, 15 ml (1 tsp) asafoetida (pound before putting in a grinder or food processor), 150 g (5½ oz) mango powder, 60 g (2¼ oz) salt, 20 g (¾ oz) ground ginger, 20 g (¾ oz) yellow or red chilli powder. Grind the cumin seeds, peppercorns, mint leaves and asafoetida together in a grinder or food processor. Transfer to a clean and dry bowl and add the remaining ingredients. Mix thoroughly, sieve and store in an airtight container in a cool, dry place.

Geelafi Seekh Kebab

An exotic and colourful kebab, full of piquant flavour.

Preparation time: 30 minutes • Cooking time: 15-20 minutes • Serves: 4-5

Ingredients

800 g (1 lb 12 oz) chicken, minced	15 ml (1 tbsp) fresh coriander, chopped
2 eggs, beaten	10 ml (2 tsp) onions, finely chopped
10 ml (2 tsp) ground cumin	55 g (2 oz) paneer, grated (page 7)
5 ml (1 tsp) yellow or red chilli powder	5 ml (1 tsp) garam masala (page 9)
5 ml (1 tsp) ground white pepper	10 ml (2 tsp) green pepper, finely chopped
Salt, to taste	
Vegetable oil	10 ml (2 tsp) tomatoes, skinned and finely chopped
55 g (2 oz) cashew nut paste (page 7)	55 g (2 oz) melted butter, for basting
20 ml (4 tsp) root ginger, peeled and chopped	5 ml (1 tsp) chaat masala (page 9)
6 green chillies, chopped	30 ml (2 tbsp) lemon juice
20 ml (4 tsp) garlic paste (page 7)	Onion rings and lemon wedges, to garnish

Method

1

Place the chicken in a bowl and add the eggs, cumin, chilli powder, white pepper, salt and oil and mix well. Set aside for 15 minutes.

2

Add the cashew nut paste, chopped ginger, chillies, garlic paste, fresh coriander, onions, grated paneer and garam masala to the chicken mixture and mix well.

3

Divide into 8 equal portions and roll into balls. Thread the meatballs on to skewers. With wet hands, spread the balls by pressing each one along the length of the skewers to make 10-cm (4-in) long kebabs, 4 cm (1½ in) apart.

4

Mix together the green pepper and tomato and gently press over the skewers evenly from top to bottom.

5

Bake in a preheated oven at 180°C/350°F/gas mark 4 for 15-20 minutes until golden brown, basting with melted butter.

6

Sprinkle with chaat masala and lemon juice, and serve garnished with onion rings and lemon wedges.

Serving suggestion

Serve with plain boiled rice or lemon rice (page 74).

Variation

Use turkey or mince in place of chicken.

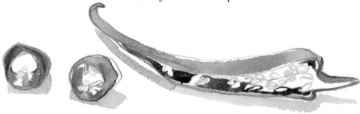

Fried Fish Patties

A deliciously light, crisp and fragrant appetiser.

Preparation time: 20 minutes • Cooking time: 20-30 minutes • Serves: 4-6

Ingredients

250 g (9 oz) skinless cod or haddock fillets	*15 ml (1 tbsp) fresh coriander, chopped*
Salt, to taste	*2.5 ml (½ tsp) black pepper*
150 g (5½ oz) fresh breadcrumbs	*2.5 ml (½ tsp) garam masala (page 9)*
1 small onion, finely chopped	*Vegetable oil, for frying*
2 green chillies, finely chopped	*Chopped fresh coriander and cream,*
5 ml (1 tsp) root ginger, peeled and finely chopped	*to garnish*

Method

1

Bring a saucepan of lightly salted water to the boil, add the fish fillets and simmer for 5-6 minutes.

2

Drain and set aside to cool.

3

Mash the fish in a bowl with the remaining ingredients, except the oil, and knead the mixture well.

4

Divide into equal-sized portions and shape into flat round patties.

5

Heat the oil in a wok (kadhai) until it is smoking. Deep-fry 4-5 patties at one time and fry until crisp and brown all over. Remove from the oil and drain on absorbent kitchen paper to remove excess oil.

6

Serve hot, garnished with chopped coriander and cream.

Serving suggestion

Serve with stir-fried okra or beans and Indian bread.

Variation

Use monkfish or salmon in place of the cod or haddock.

Chicken Tikka

A classic, easy to prepare Indian dish consisting of succulent pieces of chicken marinated in a mixture of spices, then chargrilled for extra flavour.

Preparation time: 20 minutes, plus 6 hours marinating time • Cooking time: 10 minutes • Serves: 4

Ingredients

150 ml (¼ pint) plain yogurt	*15 ml (1 tbsp) ground coriander*
5 ml (1 tsp) garlic paste (page 7)	*Salt, to taste*
7.5 ml (1½ tsp) root ginger, peeled and finely chopped	*4 boneless chicken breasts, cut into 2.5-cm (1-in) cubes*
1 small onion, grated	*Melted butter, for brushing*
7.5 ml (1½ tsp) red chilli powder	*Onion rings, tomato slices and coriander leaves, to garnish*

Method

1

Combine the yogurt, garlic paste, ginger, onion, chilli powder, coriander and salt together in a bowl and mix well. Add the chicken cubes to the marinade and coat evenly. Cover the bowl and refrigerate for at least 6 hours or overnight.

2

Skewer the chicken cubes, then cook under a preheated grill or over a charcoal grill, turning them occasionally, for 8-10 minutes or until cooked through, brushing frequently with melted butter.

3

Remove the kebabs from the skewers and place on a warmed serving dish. Garnish with onion rings, tomato slices and coriander leaves. Serve at once.

Serving suggestion

Serve with mint chutney (page 9), naan bread (page 82) and a mixed leaf salad.

Variation

Use turkey or pork in place of chicken.

Crispy Lentil Strips

A substantial vegetarian starter, this dish is also good served on its own with mint chutney (page 9).

Preparation time: 45 minutes, plus 4-5 hours soaking time • Cooking time: 25-30 minutes • Serves: 4-6

Ingredients

200 g (7 oz) split yellow lentils (chana daal)	2 green chillies, chopped
15 ml (1 tbsp) coriander seeds	Salt, to taste
15 ml (1 tbsp) black peppercorns	5 ml (1 tsp) red chilli powder
10 ml (2 tsp) root ginger, peeled and chopped	5 ml (1 tsp) garam masala (page 9)
15 ml (1 tbsp) fresh coriander, chopped	Vegetable oil, for frying

Method

1

Soak the lentils in cold water for 4-5 hours or in warm water for 30 minutes. Drain the lentils, then place them in a blender or food processor with the coriander seeds and peppercorns and grind to make a thick paste.

2

Put the paste into a large bowl, add all the remaining ingredients, except the oil, mix thoroughly and set aside for 30 minutes.

3

Heat the oil in a wok (kadhai) until it is smoking. With moist hands, shape the mixture into 10-cm (4-in) flat patties. Deep-fry the patties for 2-3 minutes on each side, then remove from the oil and drain on absorbent kitchen paper.

4

Slice the patties into 3-4 strips. Reheat the oil until it is smoking, lower the heat to medium and deep-fry the patty strips until they are crisp and golden brown all over. Drain on absorbent kitchen paper, then serve immediately.

Serving suggestion
Serve with mint chutney (page 9).

Cook's tip
Take care when preparing fresh chillies. Wear rubber gloves or wash hands thoroughly after preparing chillies, since they contain volatile oils which can irritate and burn skin and eyes.

Malai Seekh Kebab

This tasty minced lamb kebab, with herbs and cashew nuts, makes an appealing starter or cocktail snack.

Preparation time: 30 minutes • Cooking time: 15 minutes • Serves: 4

Ingredients

900 g (2 lb) minced lamb	150 g (5½ oz) shredded suet
75 g (3 oz) cashew nut paste (page 7)	45 ml (3 tbsp) vegetable oil
2 eggs, beaten	40 g (1½ oz) onions, finely chopped
10 ml (2 tsp) garam masala (page 9)	Salt, to taste
40 g (1½ oz) root ginger, peeled and finely chopped	2.5 ml (½ tsp) ground white pepper
8 green chillies, finely chopped	55 g (2 oz) butter, melted
15 ml (1 tbsp) fresh coriander, finely chopped	Onion rings, lemon wedges and shredded cabbage or carrots, to garnish

Method

1

Place all the ingredients, except the butter, in a bowl and mix well. Set aside for 15 minutes, then divide into 12 equal portions and roll into balls.

2

Preheat the oven to 200°C/400°F/gas mark 6). To make the seekh kebab, thread each ball on to a skewer. Spread by pressing each ball with a moistened palm along the length of the skewer, until each kebab is 8-10 cm (1½ in) apart.

3

Bake in a preheated oven or cook over a charcoal grill for 8-10 minutes until cooked through.

4

Remove from the oven or grill and place the skewers over a bowl to allow the excess moisture to drip off.

5

Brush with melted butter and bake or cook again for 2 minutes.

6

Remove the kebabs from the skewers on to a platter and garnish with onion rings, lemon wedges and shredded cabbage or carrots.

Serving suggestion

Serve with lemon rice (page 74) and stir-fried mushrooms.

Variation

Use beef or pork mince in place of lamb.

Mattar Kachori

These patties are crisp on the outside, with a hot, spicy filling.

Preparation time: 1¼ hours • Cooking time: 30 minutes • Makes: 18 patties

Ingredients

400 g (14 oz) plain flour	7.5 ml (1½ tsp) root ginger, peeled and finely chopped
5 ml (1 tsp) salt	Pinch of asafoetida powder
7.5 ml (1½ tsp) sugar	5 ml (1 tsp) garam masala (page 9)
75 ml (5 tbsp) clarified butter or ghee	7.5 ml (1½ tsp) lemon juice
500 g (1 lb 2 oz) peas, boiled and mashed	Pinch of baking powder
2-3 green chillies, seeded and finely chopped	Vegetable oil, for frying

Method

1

Place the flour, salt and 2.5 ml (½ tsp) sugar in a mixing bowl and stir to mix. Add 60 ml (4 tbsp) clarified butter or ghee, then rub it in with your fingertips until it is fully incorporated and the mixture resembles coarse breadcrumbs. Mix in 100 g (3½ oz) of the mashed peas. Add 105 ml (7 tbsp) chilled water and knead to form a smooth and pliable dough. Cover with plastic wrap and set aside for ½-1 hour.

2

For the filling, heat the remaining clarified butter or ghee in a pan, add the green chillies and ginger and fry for 30 seconds. Mix in the asafoetida, remaining peas, garam masala, lemon juice, baking powder and remaining sugar. Stir-fry for 1 minute. Remove from the heat and allow to cool. Divide the filling into 18 portions.

3

Divide the dough into 18 even portions. Shape each portion into a patty. Cover with a damp tea towel or plastic wrap and set aside.

4

Flatten each patty into a 6-cm (2½-in) round. Place one portion of filling in the centre of one piece of dough, then bring the sides of the dough over the filling to enclose it completely. Pinch the seams together to seal. Cover with plastic wrap or a moist tea towel. Set aside. Shape and stuff the remaining pieces of dough.

5

Heat the oil in a wok (kadhai) up to 150°C/300°F. Slip in a few patties, seam side down, at a time. Deep-fry until pale golden in colour and until they sound hollow when tapped. The crust should be delicately blistered and crisp. Drain on absorbent kitchen paper.

Serving suggestion

Serve with mint chutney (page 9) and tomato ketchup.

Variation

Use boiled, mashed broad beans in place of peas.

Rasam

This spicy lentil soup is a traditional southern Indian favourite.

Preparation time: 20 minutes • Cooking time: 15 minutes • Serves: 4

Ingredients

15 ml (1 tbsp) vegetable oil	100 g (1½ oz) split red lentils, washed and cleaned
5 ml (1 tsp) mustard seeds	
5 whole red chillies	2-3 tomatoes, skinned and quartered
10 curry leaves	3-4 black peppercorns
Pinch of asafoetida	1 green chilli, seeded and sliced
30 ml (2 tbsp) crushed garlic	100 g (3½ oz) tamarind pulp
5 ml (1 tsp) ground turmeric	Salt, to taste

Method

1

Heat the oil in a saucepan. Add the mustard seeds and cook until they begin to crackle. Add the whole red chillies, curry leaves, asafoetida and crushed garlic. Stir for a few seconds.

2

Add the turmeric, lentils, tomatoes, peppercorns, green chilli, tamarind pulp and salt.
Stir and add approximately 1 litre (1¾ pints) water.

3

Bring to the boil and simmer gently until the lentils are cooked and soft, stirring occasionally.

Paneer Dahi ke Kebab

Crispy sesame seed-coated paneer (see page 7) kebabs – a delicious vegetarian option.

Preparation time: 30 minutes • Cooking time: 15 minutes • Serves: 4

Ingredients

500 g (1 lb 2 oz) paneer (page 7), finely grated	Salt, to taste
2.5 ml (½ tsp) ground cardamom	5 ml (1 tsp) ground white pepper
10 ml (2 tsp) garam masala (page 9)	5 ml (1 tsp) yellow or red chilli powder
5 ml (1 tsp) green chillies, chopped	400 g (14 oz) plain yogurt
10 ml (2 tsp) fresh coriander, chopped	55 g (2 oz) gram flour or cornflour
2.5 ml (½ tsp) ground mace	1 egg white, lightly beaten
100 g (3½ oz) onions, finely chopped	100 g (3½ oz) sesame seeds
	100 ml (3½ oz) vegetable oil

Method

1

Place all the ingredients, except the gram flour or cornflour, egg white, sesame seeds and oil, in a bowl. Mix well with a wooden spoon and season to taste. Add the gram flour or cornflour and mix for 2 minutes.

2

Divide the mixture into 20 equal portions. Roll each portion into a ball in your palm and press slightly to form a 4-cm (1½-in) patty. Chill the patties in the refrigerator for 20 minutes. Coat each patty with egg white and sprinkle with sesame seeds.

3

Heat the oil in a deep pan or wok (kadhai), then shallow fry until golden crisp.
Alternatively, shallow fry in a non-stick frying pan. Serve hot.

Serving suggestion

Serve with cucumber slices, tomato slices, onion slices and fresh mint chutney (page 9).

Tandoori Chicken

Tender, mildly spiced grilled chicken, this is one of the most widely known
and popular dishes in the entire Indian cuisine.

Preparation time: 20 minutes, plus 5-6 hours marinating time • Cooking time: 20 minutes • Serves: 4

Ingredients

Two 600 g (1 lb 4 oz) chickens, each cut into 4 or 8 portions	10 ml (2 tsp) garam masala (page 9)
Salt, to taste	25 g (1 oz) ginger paste (page 7)
25 g (1 oz) red chilli paste (page 9)	30 ml (2 tbsp) lemon juice
10 ml (2 tsp) ginger paste (page 7)	45 ml (3 tbsp) vegetable oil
55 g (2 oz) garlic paste (page 7)	25 g (1 oz) red chilli paste (page 9)
30 ml (2 tbsp) lemon juice	Pinch of saffron
	Salt, to taste
For the marinade	200 g (7 oz) plain yogurt
5 ml (1 tsp) ground cumin	55 g (2 oz) melted butter, for brushing
	Onion rings and fresh coriander, to garnish

Method

1

Clean the chicken, remove the skin and make several incisions in each piece of chicken.

2

Mix the salt, red chilli paste, ginger and garlic pastes and lemon juice together and rub into the chicken portions.
Set aside for 30 minutes.

3

Place all the ingredients for the marinade in a bowl and whisk together until well mixed.

4

Rub the chicken portions with the marinade, cover and leave for 5-6 hours in the refrigerator.

5

Thread the chicken portions on to skewers, leaving a 4-cm (1½-in) gap between each portion. Place on a rack or baking tray.

6

Bake in a preheated oven at 180°C/350°F/gas mark 4 for approximately 15 minutes or until cooked and tender.
Brush with melted butter and bake for a further 3 minutes.

7

Arrange on a platter and serve immediately, garnished with onion rings and fresh coriander.

Cook's tips

Having made Tandoori Chicken, you can now convert it into the more exotic Murgh Khusk Parda (see page 30). Tandoori Chicken
can be served as a starter as part of a large special occasion meal, or as part of a tandoori platter mixed with other grilled meats.

Serving suggestion

Serve with a raita (page 80) and a fresh green salad.

Mughlai Kebab

These spicy lamb kebabs are ideal to cook and serve at a barbecue.

Preparation time: 20 minutes, plus 3 hours marinating time • Cooking time: 15-20 minutes • Serves: 4

Ingredients

45 ml (3 tbsp) ginger paste *(page 7)*	45 ml (3 tbsp) cheese, grated
45 ml (3 tbsp) garlic paste *(page 7)*	5 ml (1 tsp) garam masala *(page 9)*
45 ml (3 tbsp) vinegar	5 ml (1 tsp) ground cumin
10 ml (2 tsp) red chilli powder	Pinch of saffron
5 ml (1 tsp) ground black pepper	2.5 ml (½ tsp) ground fenugreek
Salt, to taste	Butter, for brushing
1 kg (2 lb 4 oz) lean boneless lamb, cut into cubes	Chopped fresh coriander, cream, lemon wedges and onion rings, to garnish
45 ml (3 tbsp) double cream	

Method

1

Mix the ginger and garlic pastes, vinegar, red chilli powder, black pepper and salt together.

2

Add the lamb, turn to coat all over, then cover and leave to marinate for 2 hours.

3

In a separate bowl, mix the cream, cheese, garam masala, cumin, saffron and fenugreek together. Add the marinated lamb to this mixture, stir to mix, then cover and set aside for 1 hour.

4

Thread the lamb on to skewers, leaving a 2-cm (¾-in) gap between the cubes. Cook in preheated oven at 180°C/350°F/gas mark 4 or over a charcoal grill for 8-10 minutes. Brush with melted butter and cook for a further 3-4 minutes until the lamb is cooked and tender.

5

Serve hot, garnished with chopped coriander, cream, lemon wedges and onion rings.

Serving suggestion

Serve on a bed of boiled brown or white rice, tossed with some chopped fresh parsley or mixed herbs.

Murgh Khusk Parda

Tandoori Chicken (page 26), bound with a light pastry covering, makes a complete meal in itself!

Preparation time: 50 minutes, plus 6 hours for the Tandoori Chicken • Cooking time: 15 minutes • Serves: 4-6

Ingredients

Tandoori Chicken (page 26)	*2 drops vetivier*
150 g (5½ oz) plain flour	*55 g (2 oz) butter, melted*
Salt, to taste	*125 ml (4 fl oz) double cream*
10 ml (2 tsp) sugar	*2 egg yolks, beaten*
100 m (3½ fl oz) milk, warmed	

Method

1

Follow the recipe for tandoori chicken on page 26 until the chicken is cooked – approximately 5 minutes.

2

Sift the flour with the salt into a mixing bowl. Dissolve the sugar in the warm milk, add the vetivier and stir to mix.

3

Pour the milk mixture on to the flour, knead into a dough and set aside for 15 minutes.

4

Add the melted butter to the dough, knead the dough again and set aside for 10 minutes.

5

Divide the dough into 2 equal portions, form each into a ball and dust with flour. Set aside for another 5 minutes.

6

Grease 2 casserole dishes, 1 for each chicken. Roll the dough out into rounds, the size of each casserole dish. Prick the surface of the dough all over with a fork.

7

Arrange the portions of 1 chicken in 1 of the casseroles. Pour half the cream over the chicken and cover with the dough (parda). Brush with beaten egg yolk.

8

Repeat this process with the remaining chicken portions and dough. Bake in a preheated oven at 180°C/350°F/gas mark 4 for 10-15 minutes, until the pastry is golden brown.

Serving suggestion

Cut open the pastry and serve the chicken along with a portion of the pastry.

Paneer Seekh Kebab

A tasty vegetarian kebab made from paneer (see page 7) and a mix of spices.

Preparation time: 15 minutes • Cooking time: 10-15 minutes • Serves: 4

Ingredients

1 kg (2 lb 4 oz) paneer (page 7), grated	*5 ml (1 tsp) ground cumin*
30 ml (2 tbsp) green chillies, chopped	*5 ml (1 tsp) red chilli powder*
2 onions, grated	*Salt, to taste*
15 ml (1 tbsp) ground ginger	*20 ml (4 tsp) cornflour*
30 ml (2 tbsp) fresh coriander, chopped	*Melted butter, for brushing*
10 ml (2 tsp) ground black pepper	

Method

1

Place all the ingredients, except the melted butter, in a large bowl and knead together until thoroughly mixed.

2

With moist hands, wrap the paneer mixture around skewers to form a kebab
approximately 10-13 cm (4-5 in) long, with a 5-cm (2-in) gap between the kebabs.

3

Cook in a preheated oven at 150°C/300°F/gas mark 2 or over a charcoal grill for 10-15 minutes,
brushing occasionally with melted butter. Serve immediately.

Serving suggestion

Serve hot, accompanied by salad and/or mint chutney (page 9).

Variation

Use tofu in place of paneer.

Mahi Tikka

A delicious way of serving white fish, which is marinated, chargrilled, then served hot.

Preparation time: 25 minutes, plus 3-4 hours marinating time • Cooking time: 15 minutes • Serves: 4

Ingredients

800 g (1 lb 12 oz) monkfish, cod or haddock fillets, cut into 4-cm (1½-in) cubes	10 ml (2 tsp) garam masala (page 9)
Salt, to taste	40 g (1½ oz) ginger paste (page 7)
20 ml (4 tsp) lemon juice	15 ml (1 tbsp) green chilli paste (page 9)
55 g (2 oz) paneer (page 7), grated	5 ml (1 tsp) ground white pepper
10 ml (2 tsp) fresh mint paste (page 9)	200 g (7 oz) plain yogurt
	55 g (2 oz) melted butter, for brushing

Method

1

Marinate the fish cubes in the salt and lemon juice for 1 hour in the refrigerator.

2

In a bowl, combine all the remaining ingredients, except the melted butter, and whisk to make a creamy batter.

3

Add the fish cubes to the batter, stir to mix, then leave to marinate for at least 2-3 hours.

4

Thread the fish cubes on to skewers, 5 pieces on each skewer, 2 cm (¾ in) apart, and cook in a preheated oven at 180°C/350°F/gas mark 4, or over an open charcoal grill for 10-12 minutes, basting occasionally with melted butter.

Serving suggestion

Serve with sliced onions, tomatoes, sliced cucumber and mint chutney (page 9).

Variation

Use oily fish such as fresh salmon or tuna in place of the white fish.

Tandoori Lobster

A spectacular party special, this lobster dish is a real treat.

Preparation time: 30 minutes, plus 4 hours marinating time • Cooking time: 10 minutes • Serves: 4

Ingredients

4 lobsters, medium-sized	1 egg
Vegetable oil	10 ml (2 tsp) garam masala (page 9)
25 g (1 oz) garlic paste (page 7)	55 g (2 oz) gram flour
25 g (1 oz) ginger paste (page 7)	45 ml (3 tbsp) mustard oil
2.5 ml (½ tsp) carom seeds	5 ml (1 tsp) red chilli paste (page 9)
125 ml (4 fl oz) malt vinegar	5 ml (1 tsp) ground white pepper
Salt, to taste	100 g (3½ oz) melted butter, for brushing
200g (7 oz) plain yogurt	Lettuce, tomatoes, onion rings and salad ingredients, to garnish
55 g (2 oz) paneer (page 7), grated	

Method

1

Cut each lobster in half, then shell and devein the lobster. Wash the shells, then dry and dip the shells into hot oil and set aside.

2

Mix together the garlic and ginger pastes, carom seeds, vinegar and salt. Add the lobster, stir to mix, then marinate for 1 hour.

3

Whisk the yogurt in a large bowl, add all the remaining ingredients, except the melted butter, and rub the lobsters with this mixture. Set aside for 3 hours.

4

Thread the lobsters onto skewers, each about 2 cm (¾ in) apart. Keep a baking tray underneath to collect any drips.

5

Bake in a preheated oven at 180°C/350°F/gas mark 4 for 5 minutes.

6

Brush with melted butter and bake for a further 2 minutes. Serve the lobster placed on the shell on a platter. Garnish with lettuce, tomatoes, onion rings and salad ingredients.

Serving suggestion

Serve with Indian bread and a mixed leaf salad.

Tandoori Jhinga

Succulent, chargrilled prawns – simple yet delicious.

Preparation time: 15 minutes, plus 3 hours marinating time • Cooking time: 20 minutes • Serves: 4

Ingredients

15 ml (1 tbsp) lemon juice	1 egg, beaten
Salt, to taste	30 ml (2 tbsp) garlic paste (page 7)
1 kg (2 lb 4 oz) king prawns	30 ml (2 tbsp) ginger paste (page 7)
2.5 ml (½ tsp) black peppercorns, crushed	10 ml (2 tsp) green chilli paste (page 9)
5 ml (1 tsp) carom seeds	Pinch of saffron, dissolved in 15 ml (1 tbsp) milk
25 g (1 oz) cornflour	
30 ml (2 tbsp) double cream	55 g (2 oz) melted butter, for brushing

Method

1

In a bowl, mix together the lemon juice and salt. Add the prawns, stir to mix and marinate for 1 hour.

2

In a separate bowl, mix together all the remaining ingredients, except the butter, and mix to a smooth batter.

3

Add the prawns to this batter, stir to mix, then marinate for 2 hours.

4

Thread the prawns onto skewers, about 2 cm (¾ in) apart. Cook in a preheated oven at 180°C/350°F/gas mark 4 or over a charcoal grill for 10 minutes.

5

Place the skewers over a bowl and allow to drain for a few minutes.

6

Brush with melted butter and bake again for 3-4 minutes. Serve.

Serving suggestion

Serve with mint chutney (page 9) and salads.

Variation

Use tiger prawns in place of king prawns.

Lamb Do Piaza

A delicious lamb curry with lots of onions, added twice, hence 'do piaza'.

Preparation time: 15 minutes • Cooking time: 50 minutes • Serves: 4

Ingredients

300 g (10½ oz) button onions	300 g (10½ oz) tomatoes, skinned, seeded and chopped
25 g (1 oz) butter	
100 ml (3½ fl oz) vegetable oil	1 kg (2 lb 4 oz) lamb, cubed
5 ml (1 tsp) ground turmeric	12.5 ml (2½ tsp) garam masala (page 9)
3 bay leaves	10 ml (2 tsp) ground coriander
10 cloves	5 ml (1 tsp) ground cumin
5 cinnamon sticks	2.5 ml (½ tsp) ground mace
8 whole red chillies	5 ml (1 tsp) ground nutmeg
10 cardamoms	10 ml (2 tsp) black peppercorns, crushed
200 g (7 oz) onions, chopped or sliced	Salt, to taste
55 g (2 oz) ginger paste (page 7)	5 ml (1 tsp) fresh coriander, chopped
55 g (2 oz) garlic paste (page 7)	5 ml (1 tbsp) ginger juliennes

Method

1
Blanch the button onions in boiling water for 2 minutes, then drain. Melt the butter in a small pan, add the onions and cook for 3 minutes, stirring. Remove from the heat and set aside.

2
Heat the oil in a pan, add the turmeric and the whole spices (bay leaves, cloves, cinnamon sticks, whole red chillies and cardamoms) and cook over a medium heat for a few seconds until they begin to crackle.

3
Add the onions and cook until soft and golden in colour. Add the ginger and garlic pastes and chopped tomatoes, stir and cook for 5 minutes.

4
Add the lamb, stir and cook for 10-15 minutes over medium heat until a pleasant aroma comes from the lamb. Reduce the heat and simmer gently for about 30 minutes until the lamb is cooked and tender, stirring occasionally.

5
Sprinkle with garam masala, coriander, cumin, mace, nutmeg and black pepper. Add salt, to taste. Add the button onions, stir, cover and cook for 2-3 minutes. Sprinkle with fresh coriander and ginger juliennes and serve.

Serving suggestion
Serve with boiled rice, naan bread (page 82) and mango chutney.

Variation
Use beef or pork in place of lamb.

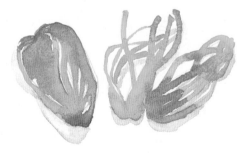

Murgh Makhani

Chicken, simmered in butter and tomato curry – a favourite recipe particularly in the north of India.

Preparation time: 15 minutes, plus time to roast the chicken if Tandoori Chicken is not available •
Cooking time: 45 minutes • Serves: 4

Ingredients

125 g (4½ oz) butter	10 ml (2 tsp) ginger juliennes
2 cinnamon sticks	5 green chillies (seeded and sliced)
10 cardamoms	5 ml (1 tsp) paprika or red chilli powder
1 bay leaf	Tandoori Chicken (page 26) (each chicken cut into 8 portions)
55 g (2 oz) ginger paste (page 7)	
55 g (2 oz) garlic paste (page 7)	150 ml (¼ pint) double cream
900 g (2 lb) tomatoes, skinned and chopped	15 ml (1 tbsp) honey
Salt, to taste	15 ml (1 tbsp) chopped fresh coriander, to garnish

Method

1
Melt half the butter in a heavy-based saucepan, add the cinnamon, cardamoms and bay leaf and cook for 30 seconds.
Stir in the ginger and garlic pastes and cook until the moisture evaporates.

2
Add the tomatoes and salt and cook until the tomatoes are soft.
Add 400 ml (14 fl oz) water, bring to the boil and simmer for 15 minutes.

3
Strain the mixture through a soup strainer into another pan.

4
Melt the remaining butter in a wok (kadhai), add the ginger juliennes and green chillies and cook for 1 minute.
Add the paprika or red chilli powder and the strained sauce and bring to the boil.

5
Add the tandoori chicken pieces and simmer for about 10 minutes or until the chicken is cooked and tender, stirring occasionally. Stir in the cream and honey.

6
Serve garnished with fresh coriander.

Serving suggestion
Serve with any Indian bread, such as paratha (page 84) or chapattis.

Rara Gosht

An easy to prepare yet delicious lamb curry.

Preparation time: 20 minutes, plus 2 hours marinating time • Cooking time: 50 minutes • Serves: 4

Ingredients

200 g (7 oz) plain yogurt	4 cardamoms
12.5 ml (2½ tsp) garlic, chopped	8 fresh whole red chillies
12.5 ml (2½ tsp) root ginger, peeled and chopped	400 g (14 oz) onions, chopped
Salt, to taste	25 g (1 oz) tomatoes, skinned and chopped
1 kg (2 lb 4 oz) lean shoulder of lamb, cubed	5 ml (1 tsp) garam masala (page 9)
100 ml (3½ fl oz) vegetable oil	15 ml (1 tbsp) chopped fresh coriander, to garnish
5 ml (1 tsp) cumin seeds	6 sliced green chillies, to garnish

Method

1

Mix together the yogurt, garlic, ginger and salt. Add the lamb, stir to mix, then leave to marinate for 2 hours.

2

Heat the oil in a frying pan. Add the cumin seeds, cardamoms and red chillies and cook for 30 seconds.

3

Add the onions and cook until golden brown, then add the tomatoes and cook for 5 minutes, stirring occasionally.

4

Add the lamb and marinade and cook until the oil separates from the sauce, stirring occasionally. Add 200 ml (7 fl oz) hot water and the garam masala, cover and simmer over a low heat for about 30-45 minutes until the lamb is cooked and tender.

5

Serve hot, garnished with fresh coriander and sliced chillies.

Serving suggestion

Serve with chapattis or paratha (page 84) and home-made mint chutney (page 9)

Variation

Use red or sweet onion in place of standard onion.

Murgh Navrattan Korma

A rich curry garnished with dried fruits.

Preparation time: 15 minutes • Cooking time: 45 minutes • Serves: 4

Ingredients

30 ml (2 tbsp) vegetable oil

25 g (1 oz) unsalted butter

1 bay leaf

5 cinnamon sticks

6 cloves

10 cardamoms

175 g (6 oz) onions, grated

25 g (1 oz) ginger paste (page 7)

25 g (1 oz) garlic paste (page 7)

5 ml (1 tsp) ground turmeric

10 ml (2 tsp) red chilli powder

100 g (3½ oz) almond paste (page 7)

Salt, to taste

20 ml (4 tsp) plain yogurt

1 kg (2 lb 4 oz) boneless chicken or chicken with bone, cut into 8 pieces

125 ml (4 fl oz) double cream

6 green chillies, cut in half

2.5 ml (½ tsp) ground mace

3 drops of vetivier

For garnishing

15 g (½ oz) pistachio nuts, chopped

25 g (1 oz) unsalted cashew nuts, chopped

10 ml (2 tsp) hazelnuts, skinned and chopped

25 (1 oz) almonds, blanched

15 g (½ oz) butter

15 g (½ oz) raisins

1.25 ml (¼ tsp) fresh ginger juliennes

2.5 ml (½ tsp) saffron strands, dissolved in 15 ml (1 tbsp) warm milk

2.5 ml (½ tsp) black cumin seed, roasted and ground

2.5 ml (½ tsp) fresh mint leaves

Method

1

For the garnish, fry the pistachio nuts, cashew nuts, hazelnuts and almonds in a little butter and set aside.

2

For the curry, heat the oil and butter in the same saucepan. Add the bay leaf, cinnamon sticks, cloves and cardamoms and cook over a medium heat until the spices begins to crackle.

3

Add the onions and cook for a few minutes. Add the ginger and garlic pastes, turmeric and red chilli powder, almond paste, salt and yogurt and cook over medium heat for 5-10 minutes, stirring until the oil separates from the mixture.

4

Add the chicken, stir and cook over a medium heat for 20-25 minutes until the chicken is cooked and tender, stirring occasionally. Add the cream, green chillies, ground mace and vetivier and stir to mix.

5

Garnish with the sautéed nuts, raisins, ginger juliennes and saffron dissolved in milk.
Sprinkle with ground cumin seed and mint leaves, and serve hot.

Serving suggestion

Serve with steamed rice.

Variation

Use turkey in place of chicken.

Vegetable Korma

A popular mixed vegetable and cashew nut curry.

Preparation time: 10 minutes • Cooking time: 20 minutes • Serves: 4

Ingredients

60 ml (4 tbsp) vegetable oil	1 bay leaf
10 cashew nuts, or almonds, blanched	5 ml (1 tsp) cumin seeds
10 raisins	8 cardamons
125 g (4½ oz) carrots, diced	40 g (1½ oz) ginger paste (page 7)
125 g (4½ oz) cauliflower, cut into small florets	40 g (1½ oz) garlic paste (page 7)
125 g (4½ oz) French beans, cut into 2-cm (¾-in) lengths	25 g (1 oz) green chilli paste (page 9)
	100 g (3½ oz) cashew nut paste (page 7)
125 g (4½ oz) peas	200 g (7 oz) plain yogurt
125 g (4½ oz) mushrooms	Salt, to taste
125 g (4½ oz) potatoes, diced	2.5 ml (½ tsp) ground white pepper
100 g (3½ oz) onions, chopped	60 ml (4 tbsp) double cream
6 cloves	5 ml (1 tsp) ginger juliennes
3 cinnamon sticks	15 ml (1 tbsp) fresh coriander, chopped

Method

1

Heat a little of the oil in a frying pan. Lightly fry the cashew nuts or almonds and the raisins, then set aside.

2

Parboil all the vegetables in a saucepan of boiling water for 5 minutes. Drain.

3

Heat the remaining oil in the frying pan. Add the cloves, cinnamon sticks, bay leaf, cumin seeds and cardamoms and cook until golden. Remove from heat and grind to a paste.

4

Add the ginger and garlic pastes, green chilli paste, cashew nut paste and the ground spice paste and cook until the oil separates from the sauce.

5

Add the yogurt and cook over a low heat for 5 minutes, stirring.

6

Add the parboiled vegetables, salt and white pepper. Cover and cook over a low heat for 5-6 minutes, stirring occasionally.

7

Stir in the cream and spoon into a serving bowl.

8

Garnish with ginger juliennes, fresh coriander and the fried dried fruit and nuts, and serve.

Serving suggestion
Serve with boiled rice and naan bread (page 82).

Variation
Choose your own selection of fresh seasonal vegetables.

Shahi Paneer

A tasty dish of paneer (page 7) curried in a creamy yogurt sauce with cashew nuts.

Preparation time: 20 minutes • Cooking time: 25-30 minutes • Serves: 4

Ingredients

75 ml (5 tbsp) vegetable oil	10 ml (2 tsp) cashew nut paste (page 7)
6 cloves	Salt, to taste
2 bay leaves	1 kg (2 lb 4 oz) paneer (page 7), cut into small cubes
3 cinnamon sticks	
6 cardamoms	175 g (6 oz) Greek yogurt
200 g (7 oz) onions, quartered, boiled and minced	125 ml (4 fl oz) double cream
40 g (1½ oz) ginger paste (page 7)	7.5 ml (1½ tsp) garam masala (page 9)
40 g (1½ oz) garlic paste (page 7)	2.5 ml (½ tsp) ground cardamon
10 ml (2 tsp) red chilli powder	2.5 ml (½ tsp) ground mace
5 ml (1 tsp) ground turmeric	3 drops of vetivier
5 ml (1 tsp) ground coriander	Pinch of saffron, dissolved in 15 ml (1 tbsp) milk

Method

1

Heat the oil in a frying pan, add the cloves, bay leaves, cinnamon and cardamoms and cook over a medium heat until they begin to crackle. Add the onions and cook for 2-3 minutes, stirring.

2

Add the ginger and garlic pastes, chilli powder, turmeric, coriander, cashew nut paste and salt. Add the paneer cubes, stir and cook for a further 5 minutes, stirring occasionally.

3

Add the yogurt and 100 ml (3½ fl oz) warm water. Bring slowly to the boil, then simmer until the oil separates from the sauce.

4

Reduce the heat, add the cream, garam masala, ground cardamom, mace, vetivier and saffron mixture and stir to mix. Serve at once.

Serving suggestion
Serve with any dry vegetable dish and Indian bread.

Variation
Use crème fraîche in place of the yogurt.

Gram Flour Dumplings in a Yogurt Curry

A hot, satisfying vegetarian dish, ideal served with boiled rice.

Preparation: 30 minutes • Cooking: 1 hour • Serves: 4

Ingredients

350 g (12 oz) plain yogurt	60 ml (4 tbsp) groundnut oil, plus extra for frying
Salt, to taste	150 g (5½ oz) potatoes, cut into rounds
5 ml (1 tsp) red chilli powder	150 g (5½ oz) onions, cut into 5-mm (¼-in) thick rounds
5 ml (1 tsp) ground turmeric	
125 g (4½ oz) gram flour	2.5 ml (½ tsp) cumin seeds
Pinch of bicarbonate of soda	1.25 ml (¼ tsp) mustard seeds
2.5 ml (½ tsp) carom seeds	1.25 ml (¼ tsp) fenugreek seeds
5 green chillies, chopped	4 whole red chillies

Method

1

Whisk the yogurt, salt, red chilli powder, turmeric and half the gram flour together in a bowl. Set aside.

2

Sift the remaining gram flour and bicarbonate of soda together, add the carom seeds and enough water to make a thick batter. Beat well. Stir in the green chillies.

3

Heat enough oil in a wok (kadhai) to deep-fry. Drop large spoonfuls of the batter into the oil to form 4-cm (1½-in) puffy dumplings. Fry until golden brown on all sides. Remove from the pan, set aside and keep warm.

4

Heat 45 ml (3 tbsp) oil in a saucepan and add the yogurt mixture and 700 ml (1¼ pints) water. Bring to the boil, reduce the heat and simmer for 8-10 minutes, stirring constantly to prevent the yogurt curdling.

5

Add the potatoes and onions and cook until the potatoes are tender. Add the dumplings, simmer for 35 minutes, stirring occasionally, then remove from the heat and transfer to a serving bowl.

6

Heat the remaining 15 ml (1 tbsp) oil in a small pan. Add the cumin, mustard and fenugreek seeds and cook until they crackle. Add the whole red chillies, remove from the heat and pour over the hot curry. Serve immediately.

Serving suggestion

Serve hot, garnished with chopped fresh coriander and accompanied by boiled white or brown rice.

Kadhai Mushroom Curry

Tender mushrooms cooked in a hot tomato curry.

Preparation time: 10 minutes • Cooking time: 15 minutes • Serves: 4

Ingredients

800 g (1 lb 12 oz) mushrooms	2.5 ml (½ tsp) ground fenugreek
60 ml (4 tbsp) vegetable oil	350 g (12 oz) tomatoes, skinned, seeded and chopped
10 whole red chillies	Salt, to taste
100 g (3½ oz) onions, chopped	10 ml (2 tsp) coriander seeds, roasted and crushed
25 g (1 oz) ginger paste (page 7)	5 ml (1 tsp) ground black pepper
25 g (1 oz) garlic paste (page 7)	6-8 sliced green chillies, to garnish
15 ml (1 tbsp) garam masala (page 9)	15 ml (1 tbsp) chopped fresh coriander, to garnish

Method

1

Trim, wash and cut the mushrooms in half. Set aside.

2

Heat the oil in a frying pan. Add the whole red chillies and chopped onions and cook for 30 seconds.
Add the ginger and garlic pastes and cook over a medium heat for 1 minute.

3

Add the garam masala, fenugreek and tomatoes and cook over a medium heat until the oil separates
from the mixture, stirring occasionally.

4

Add the mushrooms and toss over a high heat until the mushrooms are well coated in the mixture.
Cook for 5-6 minutes, stirring occasionally.

5

Season with salt and sprinkle with crushed coriander seeds and black pepper.

6

Serve immediately garnished with the green chillies and fresh coriander.

Serving suggestion

Serve with paratha (page 84) and home-made chutney.

Variation

Use shiitake or oyster mushrooms for a delicious change.

Goan Prawn Curry

This curry, made with coconut milk, embodies the true taste of Goa.

Preparation time: 20 minutes • Cooking time: 20 minutes • Serves: 4

Ingredients

1 kg (2 lb 4 oz) fresh whole prawns	15 whole red chillies
40 g (1½ oz) tamarind	100 g (3½ oz) onions, minced
25 g (1 oz) garlic paste (page 7)	150 g (5½ oz) tomatoes, skinned and chopped
25 g (1 oz) ginger paste (page 7)	Salt, to taste
5 ml (1 tsp) cumin seeds	100 ml (3½ fl oz) coconut milk
5 ml (1 tsp) ground turmeric	5 green chillies, to garnish
15 ml (1 tbsp) coriander seeds	5 ml (1 tsp) chopped fresh coriander, to garnish
125 ml (4 fl oz) vegetable oil	

Method

1

Shell, devein and pat the prawns dry.

2

Dissolve the tamarind in 100 ml (3½ fl oz) hot water for about 20 minutes. Strain all the pulp out of the tamarind.

3

Place the garlic and ginger pastes, cumin seeds, turmeric, coriander seeds and tamarind pulp into a blender.
Add 90 ml (6 tbsp) water and blend into a fine paste.

4

Heat the oil in a frying pan. Add the red chillies and cook for 30 seconds. Add the minced onions and cook over medium heat until golden brown, stirring. Add the tomatoes, salt and the blended paste and cook for 2 minutes, stirring.

5

Add half the coconut milk and 200 ml (7 fl oz) water and bring to the boil.

6

Add the prawns and cook for 5 minutes, stirring occasionally.

7

Add the remaining coconut milk and bring to the boil. Remove from the heat, garnish with green chillies and fresh coriander and serve.

Serving suggestion
Serve with boiled rice and chapattis

Variation
Use shelled mussels in place of prawns.

Kadhai Murgh Afghani

Kadhai cooking originated with this delicious hot chicken delicacy, cooked in chopped, fresh tomatoes.

Preparation time: 20 minutes • Cooking time: 30 minutes • Serves: 4

Ingredients

One 1 kg (2 lb 4 oz) chicken	*4 green chillies, chopped*
8 whole red chillies	*25 g (1 oz) root ginger, peeled and chopped*
5 ml (1 tsp) coriander seeds, roughly ground	*15 ml (1 tbsp) fresh coriander, chopped*
90 ml (6 tbsp) vegetable oil	*Salt, to taste*
25 g (1 oz) garlic paste (page 7)	*10 ml (2 tsp) garam masala (page 9)*
1 kg (2 lb 4 oz) fresh tomatoes, skinned and chopped	*5 ml (1 tsp) ground fenugreek*

Method

1

Skin the chicken and cut into 8 pieces and set aside. Grind the red chillies and coriander seeds with
a little water with a pestle and mortar to form a paste.

2

Heat the oil in a deep wok (kadhai), add the garlic paste and cook over a medium heat until it is light brown. Add the red chilli
and coriander seed mixture and the tomatoes and cook over a medium heat for 5-10 minutes, stirring occasionally.

3

Add the green chillies, ¾ of the ginger and ⅓ of the fresh coriander, reduce the heat and simmer for 4-5 minutes, stirring
frequently.

4

Add the chicken pieces and salt. Reduce the heat, cover and cook for 10-15 minutes. Stir occasionally, until the oil separates from
the mixture, the sauce becomes thick and the chicken is cooked and tender.

5

Sprinkle with garam masala, fenugreek and salt. Cook for 2 minutes, stirring.

6

Garnish with the remaining ginger and fresh coriander and serve.

Serving suggestion

Serve with steamed rice or Indian bread.

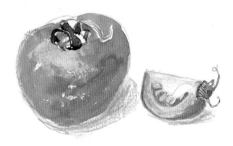

Stuffed Courgettes

This appetising dish of stuffed courgettes is quick and easy to make.

Preparation time: 30 minutes • Cooking time: 10 minutes • Serves: 2-4

Ingredients

4 courgettes, trimmed	*15 ml (1 tbsp) garam masala (page 9)*
60 ml (4 tbsp) vegetable oil, plus extra for frying	*5 ml (1 tsp) chilli powder*
	10 ml (2 tsp) dried mango powder
1 onion, finely chopped	*Salt, to taste*
2 tomatoes, skinned and chopped	*60 ml (4 tbsp) double cream*

Method

1

Wash and dry the courgettes. Slice off the top of each courgette to form a lid. Scoop out the centre and set aside.

2

Heat the oil in a frying pan and deep-fry the courgettes for 1-2 minutes. Drain off the excess oil and set aside.

3

Heat a little oil in a frying pan, add the onion and cook until transparent. Add the tomatoes,
cook for 4-5 minutes, then add the garam masala, chilli powder, mango powder and salt. Stir in the cream.
Cover and cook over a low heat for 5 minutes, stirring occasionally.

4

Fill each courgette cup with the onion mixture, replace the courgette lid, place on a baking tray and bake in a preheated
oven at 180°C/350°F/gas mark 4 for 5-7 minutes. Remove the lids and serve hot.

Serving suggestion

Serve with boiled rice and a mixed leaf salad.

Variation

Stuff other vegetables in the same way, such as peppers or mushrooms.

Kadhai Peas

A chilli hot and colourful dish. Fresh or frozen peas work equally well in this recipe.

Preparation time: 10 minutes • Cooking time: 15 minutes • Serves: 4

Ingredients

75 ml (5 tbsp) vegetable oil	900 g (2 lb) peas
25 g (1 oz) ginger paste (page 7)	Salt and freshly ground black pepper, to taste
25 g (1 oz) garlic paste (page 7)	
6 whole red chillies	5 ml (1 tsp) ground black cardamom
15 ml (1 tbsp) garam masala (page 9)	15 ml (1 tbsp) coriander seeds, crushed
10 ml (2 tsp) red chilli powder	25 ml (5 tsp) dry fenugreek leaves
15 ml (1 tbsp) lemon juice	5 green chillies, chopped
350 g (12 oz) tomatoes, skinned and chopped	15 ml (1 tbsp) fresh coriander, chopped

Method

1

Heat the oil in a wok (kadhai), add the ginger and garlic pastes and stir-fry over medium heat for 1 minute.

2

Add the whole red chillies, garam masala, red chilli powder, lemon juice and tomatoes and stir-fry for 5 minutes until the sauce is smooth and well blended.

3

Stir in the peas and cook for 5 minutes. Season with salt and pepper, stirring frequently.

4

Sprinkle the ground black cardamom, crushed coriander seeds, dry fenugreek leaves, green chillies and fresh coriander over and serve immediately.

Serving suggestion

Serve hot with Indian breads or as an accompaniment to tandoori dishes.

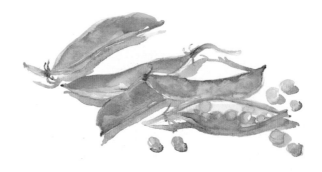

Crunchy Okra

A delicious way of cooking okra. The flavour of the dish is best when made with young, tender pods.

Preparation time: 25 minutes • Cooking time: 20 minutes • Serves: 4-6

Ingredients

500 g (1 lb 2 oz) okra (bhindi)	2.5 ml (½ tsp) chaat masala (page 9)
Salt, to taste	40 g (1½ oz) gram flour
5 ml (1 tsp) red chilli powder	Vegetable oil, for frying
5 ml (1 tsp) garam masala (page 9)	7.5 ml (1½ tsp) ginger juliennes, to garnish
2.5 ml (½ tsp) dry mango powder	2 sliced green chillies, to garnish

Method

1

Snip off both ends of each okra and slice lengthwise into four slices.

2

Spread all the sliced okra on a flat dish and sprinkle evenly with salt, chilli powder, garam masala, mango powder and chaat masala. Mix gently to coat the okra evenly.

3

Sprinkle the gram flour over the okra and mix it in so that they are coated evenly, preferably without adding any water. Divide the okra into two portions.

4

Heat the oil in a wok (kadhai) or a pan until it is smoking. Stir-fry one portion of coated okra slices, separating each lightly with a fork. Do not allow the slices to stick to each other.

5

Remove from the oil when both sides are crispy and brown in colour.

6

Fry the remaining portion of okra, as before.

7

Garnish with the ginger juliennes and green chillies and serve immediately.

Serving suggestion

Serve hot, accompanied by Indian bread.

Bharwan Shimla Mirch

These peppers stuffed with a spiced potato filling make a great vegetarian meal.

Preparation time: 50 minutes • Cooking time: 25-30 minutes • Serves: 4

Ingredients

60 ml (4 tbsp) vegetable oil	40 g (1½ oz) melted butter, for brushing
100 g (3½ oz) onions, chopped	
25 g (1 oz) cashew nuts, chopped	**For the sauce**
25 g (1 oz) raisins	30 ml (2 tbsp) vegetable oil
5 ml (1 tsp) ground white pepper	2.5 ml (½ tsp) cardamoms
7.5 ml (1½ tsp) garam masala (page 9)	1 bay leaf
10 ml (2 tsp) green chillies, finely chopped	25 g (1 oz) onions, sliced
10 ml (2 tsp) root ginger, peeled and finely chopped	3 garlic cloves, crushed
15 ml (1 tbsp) fresh coriander, chopped	300 g (10½ oz) tomatoes, skinned
Salt, to taste	2.5 ml (½ tsp) ground mace
750 g (1 lb 10 oz) potatoes, boiled and mashed	Salt, to taste
10 green peppers, each weighing approximately 70 g (2½ oz)	60 ml (4 tbsp) double cream

Method

1

Heat the oil in a frying pan and cook the onions, cashew nuts and raisins over a medium heat for 5-6 minutes.

2

Add the white pepper, garam masala, green chillies, ginger, half of the fresh coriander and salt.
Add the potatoes and cook for 5 minutes, stirring. Remove the pan from the heat.

3

Fill each pepper with the potato mixture and arrange the peppers in a greased baking dish.
Bake in a preheated oven at 180°C/350°F/gas mark 4 for 25-30 minutes. Brush occasionally with melted butter.

4

To make the sauce, heat the oil in a saucepan, add the cardamoms, bay leaf, onions,
garlic cloves, tomatoes and 400 ml (14 fl oz) water and cook for 30 minutes, stirring occasionally.
Strain the sauce through a fine sieve. Stir in the mace, salt and cream.

5

Remove the peppers from the oven and arrange them on a platter.
Pour the sauce over the peppers, sprinkle with the remaining fresh coriander and serve.

Serving suggestion

Serve with boiled mixed brown and wild rice.

Variation

Stuff other vegetables such as courgettes or aubergines in place of the peppers.

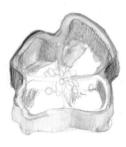

Stir-Fried Mushrooms

An excellent vegetable dish to serve as an accompaniment to a curry, or as a light meal or snack with Indian breads.

Preparation time: 10 minutes • Cooking time: 20 minutes • Serves: 4

Ingredients

500 g (1 lb 2 oz) mushrooms	*2.5 ml (½ tsp) ground turmeric*
20 ml (4 tsp) vegetable oil	*2.5 ml (½ tsp) garam masala (page 9)*
2 onions, sliced	*2.5 ml (½ tsp) red chilli powder*
5 ml (1 tsp) garlic paste (page 7)	*Salt, to taste*
1 tomato, skinned and chopped	*15 ml (1 tbsp) fresh coriander, chopped*

Method

1
Cut the mushrooms into slices.

2
Heat the oil in a frying pan and fry the onions until golden in colour. Add the garlic paste and tomatoes, mixing well.

3
Add the turmeric, garam masala, chilli powder and salt and stir-fry for 3-4 minutes. Stir in the mushrooms and simmer until the mushrooms are tender, adding a little water if necessary and stirring occasionally.

4
Sprinkle with chopped coriander and serve hot.

Serving suggestion
Serve with naan bread (page 82) or paratha (page 84).

Variation
Use a mixture of mushrooms, such as button, brown cap and wild (shiitake or oyster).

Crispy Cauliflower

Cauliflower, deep-fried in a spicy batter, is wonderfully crisp and flavourful.

Preparation: 15 minutes • Cooking: 15 minutes • Serves: 4

Ingredients

5 small whole cauliflowers weighing about 1 kg (2 lb 4 oz) in total	20 ml (4 tsp) green chillies, finely chopped
Salt, to taste	100 g (3½ oz) plain yogurt
10 ml (2 tsp) ground turmeric	10 ml (2 tsp) ginger paste (page 7)
200 g (7 oz) gram flour	10 ml (2 tsp) garlic paste (page 7)
5 ml (1 tsp) carom seeds	10 ml (2 tsp) garam masala (page 9)
2.5 ml (½ tsp) lemon juice	10 ml (2 tsp) red or yellow chilli powder
30 ml (2 tbsp) fresh coriander, finely chopped	500 ml (18 fl oz) vegetable oil

Method

1

Boil sufficient water to immerse the whole cauliflowers. Add 5 ml (1 tsp) salt and the ground turmeric.

2

Add the cauliflowers to the water. Cook for 8-10 minutes over a medium heat until the cauliflowers are half cooked. Drain and set aside.

3

Prepare a batter by mixing the gram flour, carom seeds, lemon juice, coriander, green chillies, yogurt, ginger and garlic pastes, garam masala, chilli powder, salt and just enough water to make a thick and smooth consistency.

4

Heat the oil in a wok (kadhai). Dip each cauliflower into the batter to coat evenly and deep-fry over a medium heat until golden and crisp.

Serving suggestion
Serve hot, accompanied by mint chutney (page 9).

Variation
Use broccoli florets in place of the cauliflower.

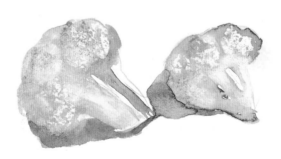

Dum Alu Bhojpuri

Mildly spiced, stuffed potatoes make an unusual vegetable dish.

Preparation time: 20 minutes • Cooking time: 20 minutes • Serves 4

Ingredients

15 ml (1 tbsp) clarified butter or ghee	*45 ml (3 tbsp) vegetable oil*
85 g (3 oz) onions, grated	
30 ml (2 tbsp) ginger paste (page 7)	**For the sauce**
30 ml (2 tbsp) garlic paste (page 7)	*1 bay leaf*
200 g (7 oz) potatoes, boiled and grated	*2 cinnamon sticks*
10 ml (2 tsp) red chilli powder	*6 cloves*
5 ml (1 tsp) ground turmeric	*6 cardamoms*
10 ml (2 tsp) garam masala (page 9)	*2.5 ml (½ tsp) black cumin seeds*
15 ml (1 tbsp) lemon juice	*150 g (5½ oz) plain yogurt*
Salt, to taste	*Chopped fresh coriander, ginger juliennes*
600 g (1 lb 4 oz) small potatoes	*and cream, to garnish*

Method

1

Heat the clarified butter or ghee in a pan, add 25 g (1 oz) of grated onions, 15 ml (1 tbsp) each of the ginger and garlic pastes and cook for 4-5 minutes. Add the boiled, grated potatoes, 5 ml (1 tsp) of the chilli powder, turmeric and garam masala. Season with a little of the lemon juice and salt. Set aside.

2

Boil the small potatoes in a saucepan of boiling water until cooked. Drain. Scoop out the flesh from the potatoes.

3

Fry the potato cases in a little of the oil, then stuff each potato with the potato mixture from Step 1. Cover and set aside.

4

Heat the remaining oil in a frying pan over a medium heat. Add the bay leaf, cinnamon sticks, cloves, cardamoms and black cumin seeds and fry for 30-50 seconds or until they begin to crackle.

5

Add the remaining grated onions and ginger and garlic pastes and fry for 2-3 minutes. Add the remaining red chilli powder and turmeric and fry over a medium heat for 5-6 minutes, stirring occasionally.

6

Add the yogurt. Stir and cook until the moisture evaporates. Add 2.5 ml (½ tsp) of the remaining garam masala and season to taste with salt.

7

Arrange the stuffed potatoes carefully in the bottom of a saucepan. Sprinkle with the remaining garam masala and lemon juice. Cover and cook for 3-4 minutes on a very low heat.

8

Transfer to a serving platter and garnish with chopped coriander, ginger juliennes and drizzle with fresh cream.

Serving suggestion
Serve with rice or Indian bread.

Variation
Use sweet potatoes in place of standard potatoes.

Lemon Rice

A deliciously fragrant way to serve rice and a tasty alternative to plain boiled rice.

Preparation time: 15 minutes • Cooking time: 40 minutes • Serves: 4

Ingredients

100 g (3½ oz) rice, basmati or any long-grain variety of rice	5 ml (1 tsp) mustard seeds
	2-3 whole red chillies
5 ml (1 tsp) salt	2.5 ml (½ tsp) ground turmeric
45 ml (3 tbsp) vegetable oil, clarified butter or ghee	75 ml (5 tbsp) lemon juice
75 g (2¾ oz) cashew nuts, chopped	40 g (1½ oz) fresh coriander, coarsely chopped
10 g (¼ oz) split red lentils	25 g (1 oz) fresh coconut, shredded

Method

1

Wash and soak the rice in water for 10 minutes. Drain and set aside.

2

Bring 450 ml (16 fl oz) water to boil in a heavy saucepan. Stir in the rice, salt and 10 ml (2 tsp) of the oil. Cover tightly, reduce the heat and simmer without stirring until the rice is fluffy and tender and the water is all absorbed. Set aside.

3

Heat the remaining oil in a small saucepan, add the cashew nuts and stir-fry until golden brown. Place on absorbent kitchen paper to absorb the excess oil, then spoon the cashew nuts over the cooked rice. Replace the lid and set aside.

4

Increase the heat slightly, add the lentils and mustard seeds to the small pan and cook until the lentils turn reddish brown and the mustard seeds splutter. Add the whole red chillies and remove the pan from the heat.

5

Gently fold the lentil mixture, turmeric, lemon juice, coriander and coconut into the cooked rice until well mixed. Serve immediately.

Serving suggestion

Serve hot, accompanied by plain yogurt and poppadoms.

Variation

Use hazelnuts or almonds in place of cashew nuts.

Broccoli and Carrot Pulao

A colourful rice accompaniment for meat or vegetable curries.

Preparation time: 15 minutes • Cooking time: 30 minutes • Serves: 4

Ingredients

400 g (14 oz) basmati rice	5 ml (1 tsp) black peppercorns
30 ml (2 tbsp) vegetable oil	150 g (5½ oz) broccoli florets
7.5 ml (1½ tsp) cumin seeds	100 g (3½ oz) carrots, diced and parboiled
1 bay leaf	Salt, to taste
3 cloves	1 litre (1¾ pints) water

Method

1
Clean, wash and soak the rice in water for 10 minutes. Drain and set aside.

2
Heat the oil in a heavy-based saucepan, add the cumin seeds, bay leaf, cloves and black peppercorns and cook until they crackle.
Add the broccoli, carrots and salt and stir-fry for 3-4 minutes.

3
Remove and discard the whole spices and set the vegetables aside.

4
Bring the water to boil in a separate pot. Add the rice, cover and cook for 25 minutes until tender. Drain.

5
Gently fold the cooked vegetables into the rice and transfer to a serving platter. Serve hot.

Serving suggestion
Serve with a light vegetable curry dish, such as Kadhai Mushroom Curry on page 54.

Variation
Use cauliflower florets in place of broccoli.

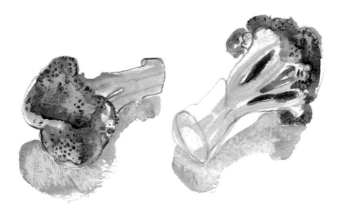

Daal Makhani

A filling side dish, ideal served with Indian bread.

Preparation time: 15 minutes, plus 3-7 hours soaking time • Cooking time: approximately 3 hours • Serves: 4

Ingredients

300 g (10½ oz) whole black lentils (black urad daal)	150 g (5½ oz) tomato purée
125 g (4½ oz) butter	Salt, to taste
20 ml (4 tsp) ginger paste (page 7)	5 ml (1 tsp) chilli powder
20 ml (4 tsp) garlic paste (page 7)	10 ml (2 tsp) fresh coriander, chopped
2 green chillies, sliced	150 ml (¼ pint) double cream

Method

1

Soak the lentils in cold water for at least 3 hours or overnight.

2

Cook the lentils in 1.5 litres (2¾ pints) boiling water over a low heat until the grains split. Stir to mash them, then set aside.

3

Heat the butter and fry the ginger and garlic pastes for 1 minute. Add the green chillies, tomato purée, salt and chilli powder. Cook for 2-3 minutes, then stir in the cooked lentils, coriander and cream, leaving 15 ml (1 tbsp) aside. Cook for a further 10-15 minutes, stirring occasionally.

4

Serve hot, garnished with a swirl of the reserved cream.

Serving suggestion

Serve with Indian bread such as naan (page 82), paratha (page 84) or chapattis.

Mixed Raita

A mildly spiced yogurt dish that brings a refreshing, cooling note to any Indian meal.

Preparation time: 30 minutes • Serves: 4

Ingredients

5 ml (1 tsp) cumin seeds	25 g (1 oz) tomatoes, skinned and chopped
5 ml (1 tsp) coriander seeds	
2.5 ml (½ tsp) black peppercorns	5 ml (1 tsp) mint, chopped
600 g (1 lb 5 oz) plain yogurt	Pinch of red chilli powder
25 g (1 oz) cucumber, chopped	Salt, to taste
25 g (1 oz) onion, chopped	Whole dried or fresh chillies and curry leaves, to garnish (optional)
5 ml (1 tsp) green chillies, finely chopped	

Method

1

Heat a griddle or heavy-based frying pan over low heat and dry roast the cumin and coriander seeds and black peppercorns, stirring, until they give off a strong aroma. Allow the seeds to cool, then crush them with a pestle and mortar.

2

Place the yogurt in a medium bowl and beat until smooth, if necessary. Stir in the chopped cucumber, onion, green chillies, tomatoes, mint, chilli powder and salt to taste.

3

Turn into a serving dish, stir in ¾ of the crushed spices and chill. Before serving, sprinkle with the remaining spice mixture and garnish with whole dried or fresh chillies and curry leaves, if you like.

Serving suggestion

Serve with chapattis or naan (page 82) and serve with chilli-hot curries and kebabs.

Variation

Use 55 g (2 oz) chopped banana in place of the tomatoes.

Naan

This leavened bread is ideal for mopping up the sauce and juices of any Indian dish.

Preparation time: 3 hours • Cooking time: 20 minutes • Serves: 6

Ingredients

500 g (1 lb 2 oz) plain flour	10 ml (2 tsp) sugar
Salt, to taste	50 ml (2 fl oz) milk
1.25 ml (¼ tsp) bicarbonate of soda	25 g (1 oz) vegetable oil or clarified butter or ghee
5 ml (1 tsp) baking powder	2.5 ml (½ tsp) onion seeds
1 egg	5 ml (tsp) melon seeds

Method

1

Sift the flour, salt, bicarbonate of soda and baking powder into a bowl. Add enough water to make a firm dough.

2

Break the egg into a bowl and add the sugar and milk. Whisk together, then gradually add the egg mixture to the dough. Knead to make a soft but smooth dough, cover with a moist cloth and set aside for 10 minutes.

3

Add the oil, knead and punch the dough, cover with a moist cloth and set aside for 2 hours to allow the dough to rise.

4

Divide the dough into 6 portions. Form each piece of dough into a ball and place on a lightly floured surface. Sprinkle with the onion and melon seeds, flatten the balls slightly, then cover and set aside for 5 minutes.

5

Flatten each ball between the palms of your hands to make rounds approximately 3 mm (⅛ in) thick and 5 cm (2 in) in diameter, then stretch on one side to make the shape of an elongated oval.

6

Place the naan on a greased baking tray and bake in a preheated oven at 180°C/350°F/gas mark 4 for 2-3 minutes. Serve immediately.

Paratha

The perfect accompaniment for any Indian meal.

Preparation time: 20 minutes • Cooking time: 10 minutes • Makes: 5

Ingredients

500 g (1 lb 2 oz) plain wholemeal flour

Salt, to taste

200 g (7 oz) clarified butter or ghee, melted

Method

1

Sift the flour and salt into a bowl, add 30 ml (2 tbsp) clarified butter or ghee, then gradually add 250 ml (9 fl oz) water and knead to a smooth dough.

2

Divide into 5 equal portions and shape into balls. Dust with flour, cover and set aside for 10 minutes.

3

Flatten each ball of dough and roll out. Brush with clarified butter or ghee and fold over. Brush the folded surface with clarified butter or ghee and fold over again to form a triangle. Roll out the triangle with a rolling pin.

4

Heat a griddle and brush the surface with clarified butter or ghee. Place the paratha on the griddle and cook for a few minutes. Coat with a little clarified butter or ghee, turn over and cook on the other side. Both sides of the paratha should be crisp and delicately browned.

5

Remove from the griddle and serve immediately.

Serving suggestion

Serve with a lamb curry or Vegetable Korma (page 48) and mango chutney.

Variation

Use a mixture of wholemeal and white flour.

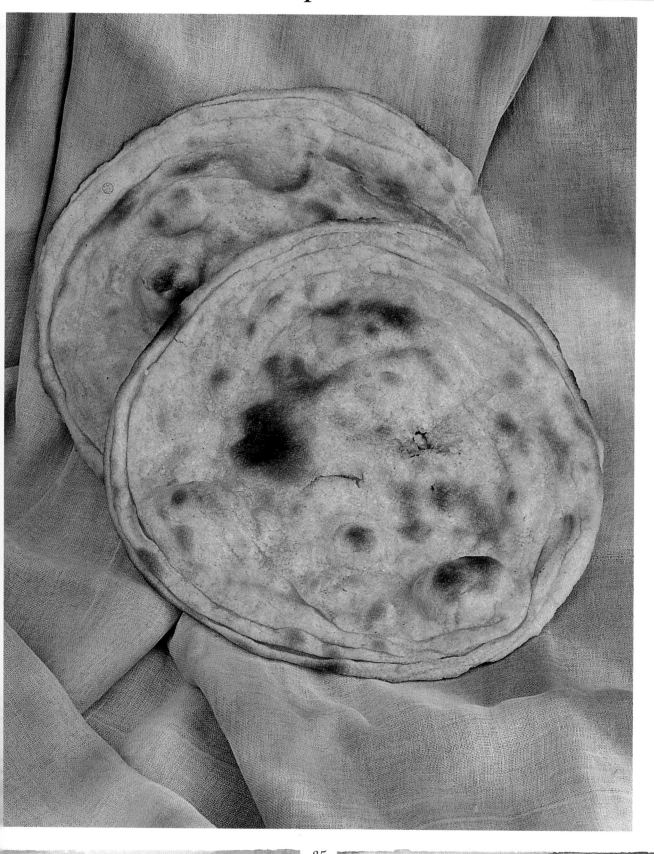

Rajbhog

An appealing dessert, ideal served with fresh sliced fruits or a fruit compôte.

Preparation time: 50 minutes • Cooking time: 2-3 hours • Serves: 8

Ingredients

For the filling	For the chenna dumplings
325 ml (11 fl oz) milk	2 litres (3½ pints) milk
30 ml (2 tbsp) caster sugar	60 ml (4 tbsp) lemon juice, strained
40 g (1½ oz) pistachio nuts, grated	1.5 kg (3 lb 5 oz) granulated sugar
5 cardamoms, crushed	15 ml (1 tbsp) cornflour, dissolved in 30 ml (2 tbsp) water
	A few drops of rose water

Method

1

For the filling, place the milk and sugar in a heavy-based saucepan, bring to the boil, then simmer until reduced by half.
Reduce the heat, add the nuts and cardamoms and cook until the mixture pulls away from the sides of the pan.
Scrape the paste onto a plate and set aside to cool.

2

For the chenna dumplings, heat the milk in a saucepan over high heat and bring to a frothing boil, stirring constantly. Reduce the
heat and add the lemon juice to make the milk curdle and the cheese to separate from the whey. If it does not, then add another
15 ml (1 tbsp) lemon juice. Remove from the heat and set aside to cool.

3

Pour the cheese-whey mixture into a moist cheese cloth. Gather the 4 corners of the cloth and rinse under running tap water for
10 minutes. Gently twist the cloth to squeeze out any excess water. Tie the corners and hang for 20-45 minutes to allow to drain.

4

Meanwhile, place the sugar in a pan with 2 litres (3½ pints) water. Cook gently, stirring, until the sugar dissolves.
Increase the heat and cook for a further 5 minutes. Remove from the heat and set aside.

5

Unwrap the cheese on a clean work surface and crumble it repeatedly until it becomes fluffy and even.
Divide into 8 balls and flatten into patties approximately 3 cm (1¼ in) in diameter.
Divide the filling into 8 portions, place one in the centre of each patty and roll to form seamless balls.

6

Reheat the sugar syrup, bring to the boil and slide in the prepared balls. Increase the heat and boil continuously
for about 20 minutes, adding the cornflour with 50 ml (2 fl oz) water after 4 minutes of boiling.
Thereafter, add 50 ml (2 fl oz) water after every 4 minutes to maintain the consistency of the syrup.
Take care to add the water directly into the syrup and not on the balls. Remove from the heat.

7

Allow to cool for 10 minutes, then add the rose water. Leave the dumplings to soak at room temperature
for at least 4 hours before serving. Serve chilled or at room temperature.

Serving suggestion
Serve with kulfi (Indian ice cream) or fresh fruits such as mango and guava.

Variation
Use almonds in place of pistachios.

Shahi Tukda

An exotic dessert which originated from the court of the nawabs.

Preparation time: 20 minutes • Cooking time: 50 minutes • Serves: 4

Ingredients

10 slices white bread, cut into 2-cm (¾-in) slices	1.25 ml (¼ tsp) saffron, dissolved in 15 ml (1 tbsp) warm milk
150 g (5½ oz) clarified butter or ghee	**For the sugar syrup**
1 litre (1¾ pints) full cream milk	
300 g (10½ oz) caster sugar	60 g (2¼ oz) granulated sugar
25 g (1 oz) chopped pistachio nuts, to garnish	4 drops rose water

Method

1

To prepare the sugar syrup, place the sugar and 200 ml (7 fl oz) water in a saucepan. Heat gently, stirring, until the sugar has dissolved, then bring to the boil. Boil rapidly until half the quantity of liquid is left. From time to time, remove any scum from the surface. Cool the syrup and stir in the rose water.

2

Remove the crusts from each slice of bread. Heat the clarified butter or ghee in a frying pan and fry the bread slices until golden on both sides. (These are the tukdas.)

3

Soak these tukdas in the cooled syrup.

4

Bring the milk to the boil over a medium heat. Simmer the milk (uncovered) for 30-45 minutes until its consistency is slightly thick and its colour is a pale yellow. Gradually stir in the sugar.

5

Cook for a further 3-4 minutes, until the sugar is completely dissolved. (This milk concentrate is called rabri.)

6

Cool, then chill.

7

Arrange each fried tukda on a platter. Pour the chilled rabri over the fried tukdas. Garnish with chopped pistachio nuts and drizzle with saffron milk. Serve immediately.

Cook's tip

Hot rabri may also be used to top the tukda instead of chilled rabri.

Serving suggestion

Serve with a selection of fresh, exotic fruits.

Gajar ka Halwa

A tasty dessert, especially delicious served hot.

Preparation time: 10 minutes • Cooking time: 1 hour • Serves: 10-12

Ingredients

1 kg (2 lb 4 oz) carrots, washed, peeled and grated	30 ml (2 tbsp) almonds, blanched, sliced or slivered
600 ml (1 pint) milk	40 g (1½ oz) raisins
115 g (4 oz) caster sugar	40 g (1½ oz) walnuts, chopped
85 g (3 oz) soft brown sugar	1.25 ml (¼ tsp) ground cloves
5 ml (1 tsp) ground cardamom	1.25 ml (¼ tsp) ground nutmeg
75 ml (5 tbsp) melted butter or vegetable oil	1.25 ml (¼ tsp) ground cinnamon

Method

1

Place the carrots and milk in a saucepan and bring to the boil. Reduce the heat to medium and cook for 20-25 minutes, stirring continuously until the mixture is nearly dry.

2

Add the caster sugar, brown sugar and half the cardamom. Cook for 10-12 minutes, stirring. Remove the pan from the heat and set aside.

3

Heat the butter or oil in a pan over a medium heat and fry the almonds until golden. Stir in the carrot mixture, raisins, walnuts and ground spices. Cook until the mixture begins to separate from the sides, stirring occasionally. Serve hot, garnished with the remaining cardamom.

Serving suggestion

Serve on its own or with kulfi (Indian ice cream), or wafer or sponge biscuits.

Variation

Use pistachio nuts in place of the almonds.

Lavang Latika

These crisp-fried parcels enclose an aromatic, clove-spiced nut filling.

Preparation time: 1 hour • Cooking time: 10 minutes • Serves: 4

Ingredients

200 g (7 oz) plain flour, sifted	2.5 ml (½ tsp) ground cloves
30 ml (2 tbsp) vegetable oil	30 ml (2 tbsp) icing sugar
A few strands of saffron, soaked in 15 ml (1 tbsp) water	12 cloves
	Vegetable oil, for frying

For the filling

125 g (4½ oz) khoya (see recipe below), mashed
25 g (1 oz) almonds, slivered
25 g (1 oz) pistachio nuts, slivered

For the sugar syrup

500 g (1 lb 2 oz) granulated sugar
700 ml (1¼ pints) water

Method

1

Place the flour in a bowl and make a well in the centre.

2

Add the oil and saffron and incorporate into the flour.

3

Gradually add 60 ml (4 tbsp) water and knead to make a firm dough. Cover with a wet cloth and allow to rest for 15 mintues.

4

For the filling, mix together the khoya, almonds, pistachio nuts, cloves and icing sugar. Divide into 12 equal portions.

5

For the sugar syrup, place the sugar and water in a pan and heat until the sugar is completely dissolved.
Bring to the boil and simmer for 2-3 minutes.

6

Divide the dough into 12 equal portions and shape into balls. Roll out each of these balls into pancakes 15 cm (6 in) in diameter

7

Place one portion of filling in the centre of each pancake and brush the edges with water.

8

Fold the pancakes from the right edge to the centre and press firmly to seal in the filling.
Repeat from the left edge, to give a 5-cm (2-in) wide strip.

9

Keeping the folded side out, make a ring with the strip. Brush the edges with water and press firmly to seal. Secure with a clove.

10

Heat a little oil in a frying pan and shallow fry over a very low heat for 8-10 minutes until crisp and golden brown in colour.
Remove and drain on absorbent kitchen paper to remove excess oil.

11

Dip in the hot sugar syrup to submerge completely, turning gently if required. Allow to soak for 2-3 minutes.
Remove and drain to remove the excess syrup.

12

Arrange neatly on a serving dish and serve.

Serving suggestion

Serve with kulfi (Indian ice cream) or a platter of fresh, sliced fruits.

To make khoya

Boil 2 litres (3½ pints) milk in a wok (kadhai). Simmer until the quantity is reduced by half, stirring occasionally.
Continue cooking, stirring constantly and scraping the milk from the pan sides, until a thick paste-like consistency is obtained
(this can take 1-1½ hours). Allow to cool before using.

Besan Ladoo

Quick and easy to make, this dessert keeps well for up to 15 days, if stored in airtight container.

Preparation time: 10 minutes • Cooking time: 20 minutes • Makes: 24 balls

Ingredients

175 ml (6 fl oz) unsalted butter or vegetable oil	*30 ml (2 tbsp) walnuts, chopped*
	Pinch of ground nutmeg
200 g (7 oz) gram flour, sifted	*115 g (4 oz) granulated sugar*
30 ml (2 tbsp) coconut, dried and grated	*Slivered nuts, to garnish*

Method

1

Melt the butter or oil in a heavy-based saucepan over a low heat. Add the gram flour, coconut, walnuts and nutmeg and cook for about 5 minutes, stirring continuously. Add the sugar and continue to cook for 10-15 minutes or until the mixture is thick and deep golden brown, stirring.

2

When cool enough to handle, turn onto a clean flat surface and shape into 24 equal-sized balls.

3

Garnish with slivered nuts and serve at room temperature.

Serving suggestion

Serve with fresh, sliced fruits such as pineapple, mango, guava, bananas and melon.

Variation

Use soft brown or demerara sugar in place of the white sugar.

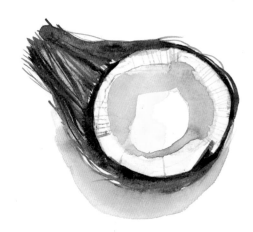

Index